The **INSIDE GUIDE**

CELEBRATING HISPANIC CULTURES

Celebrating the People of

Cuba

By Rosie Banks

Cavendish
Square

New York

Published in 2023 by Cavendish Square Publishing, LLC
29 E. 21st Street New York, NY 10010

Website: cavendishsq.com

This publication represents the opinions and views of the author based on his or her personal experience, knowledge, and research. The information in this book serves as a general guide only. The author and publisher have used their best efforts in preparing this book and disclaim liability rising directly or indirectly from the use and application of this book.

Disclaimer: Portions of this work were originally authored by Melissa Raé Shofner and published as *The People and Culture of Cuba* (Celebrating Hispanic Diversity). All new material this edition authored by Rosie Banks.

All websites were available and accurate when this book was sent to press.

Library of Congress Cataloging-in-Publication Data

Names: Banks, Rosie, 1978- author.
Title: Celebrating the people of Cuba / Rosie Banks.
Description: New York : Cavendish Square Publishing, [2023] | Series: The Inside Guide: Celebrating Hispanic Cultures | Includes index.
Identifiers: LCCN 2021040426 (print) | LCCN 2021040427 (ebook) | ISBN 9781502664549 (hardcover) | ISBN 9781502664525 (paperback) | ISBN 9781502664532 (set) | ISBN 9781502664556 (ebook)
Subjects: LCSH: Cuba–Juvenile literature.
Classification: LCC F1758.5 .B27 2023 (print) | LCC F1758.5 (ebook) | DDC 972.91–dc23
LC record available at https://lccn.loc.gov/2021040426
LC ebook record available at https://lccn.loc.gov/2021040427

Editor: Therese Shea
Copyeditor: Jill Keppeler
Designer: Deanna Paternostro

The photographs in this book are used by permission and through the courtesy of: Cover Lena Wurm/Shutterstock.com; p. 4 simonovstas/Shutterstock.com; pp. 6-7 Christian_Schmidt/Shutterstock.com; pp. 8-9, 24 akturer/Shutterstock.com; p. 10 Everett Collection/Shutterstock.com; p. 12 emkaplin/Shutterstock.com; p. 14 Harold Escalona/Shutterstock.com; p. 16 Kamira/Shutterstock.com; p. 19 bonchan/Shutterrstock.com; p. 20 phototim/Shutterstock.com; pp. 21, 29 (center) Kobby Dagan/Shutterstock.com; p. 22 Studio MDF/Shutterstock.com; p. 25 Maurizio De Mattei/Shutterstock.com; p. 26 Galina Savina/Shutterstock.com; p. 27 diy13/Shutterstock.com; p. 28 (flag) Randall Skeffington/Shutterstock.com; p. 28 (map) Andrei Minsk/Shutterstock.com; p. 29 (left) Julia-Bogdanova/Shutterstock.com; p. 29 (right) Milosz Maslanka/Shutterstock.com.

Some of the images in this book illustrate individuals who are models. The depictions do not imply actual situations or events.

CPSIA compliance information: Batch #CS23CSQ: For further information contact Cavendish Square Publishing LLC, New York, New York, at 1-877-980-4450.

Printed in the United States of America

Find us on

CONTENTS

The main island of Cuba is the largest island in the Caribbean Sea.

WELCOME TO CUBA

Cuba is a country in the West Indies that's located about 100 miles (161 kilometers) south of Key West, Florida. It's made up of more than 1,000 islands altogether. The main island is 777 miles (1,250 km) long and 119 miles (191 km) across at its widest point. It's only 19 miles (31 km) across at its narrowest point.

Cuba is a Spanish-speaking country, so its inhabitants (as well as Cubans living in other countries) are sometimes described as Hispanic. Its culture is a mix of African, European, and native islander influences, but many Cubans have a Spanish background. The rich **heritage** of Cuba can be experienced through the country's food, religion, art, music, and much more. The country's political history has also played a large role in shaping its culture.

Fast Fact

Tourism has become one of the major parts of the Cuban economy. Beautiful beaches and a warm climate attract millions of visitors each year.

The Landscape

Cuba is an archipelago, which means it's a group of many islands. The exact number is somewhere around 1,600 islands, **islets**, and **cays**. When viewed from high above, the main island looks like a crocodile. In fact,

LATINO OR HISPANIC?

Cuba is usually included as part of Latin America. So are Cubans Hispanics, Latinos, or something else? These terms are often confused. "Latino," "Latina," and the **gender-neutral** term "Latinx" describe a person living in the United States whose ancestors are from Latin America, including the country of Brazil (where people speak Portuguese, not Spanish). Because of this, Cuban Americans might call themselves "Latinos," while Cuban citizens might use "Hispanic." Some people don't use any of these terms. It's important to honor the exact language people prefer. It's a sign of respect to ask them if you don't know.

some people refer to Cuba in Spanish as *El Cocodrilo* ("The Crocodile").

Cuba's landscape includes jungles, grasslands, deserts, and forests. About one-fourth of the island is covered with hills or mountains, and much of the rest is plains.

Rounded hills called mogotes are scattered across Viñales Valley, located at the western end of Cuba.

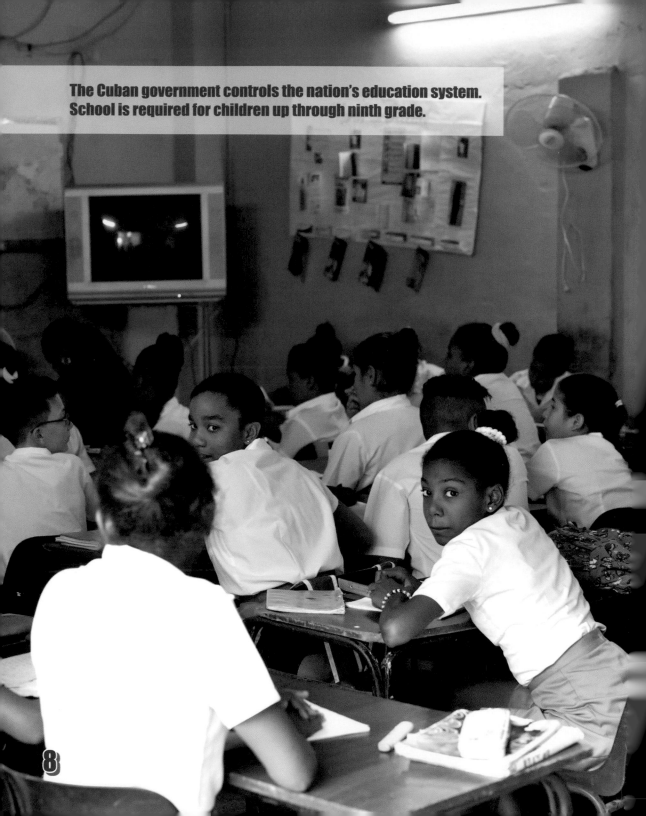

The Cuban government controls the nation's education system. School is required for children up through ninth grade.

The island's climate is tropical, and the average temperature is about 79 degrees Fahrenheit (26 degrees Celsius). Hurricanes are most likely there between June and November.

Sugarcane and tobacco are Cuba's most important crops. Cuban cigars are famous around the world for their quality. However, smoking them is bad for a person's health. Coffee, zinc, and nickel are also important exports.

Cuban Culture

The culture of Cuba is different from that of other Hispanic countries but just as rich. Traditions reflect the nation's historical connection to Spain but also a great deal of African influence, which can especially be observed in Cuban dancing, art, and music.

Before 1959, Cuba's largest cities served as its cultural centers. After the 1959 Cuban Revolution, however, the new government had positive and negative effects on the country's culture. It limited artists' freedom to express themselves but also spread cultural institutions across the island. A government agency called the Ministry of Culture was set up in 1976. The Ministry of Culture oversaw the establishment of about 250 museums and 2,000 libraries. Cubans were given greater access to music, theater, art, and dance.

This is a depiction of the Battle of Las Guasimas in the Spanish-American War. It was a victory for Cubans and Americans.

A TROUBLED HISTORY

Studying Cuba's past is essential to understand its current culture. The first peoples to live in Cuba were likely the Ciboney and Guanahatabey, hunter-gatherers who occupied the western part. The Taíno people, who were farmers, made their homes throughout the rest of the main island. Likely around 75,000 **indigenous** peoples lived on the island when Europeans arrived.

In 1492, Christopher Columbus landed on and claimed Cuba for Spain. Spanish settlers began arriving in 1511. They brought enslaved Africans to grow and harvest sugarcane. They also brought warfare and diseases that killed many of the native peoples.

Into the 20th Century

The Spanish were forced out of Cuba following the Spanish-American War of 1898. While Cuba became independent from Spain, the United States remained involved in the country's affairs. In 1902, the **Republic** of Cuba was established. The new government was weak, and many people lived in poverty.

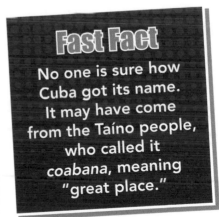

Fast Fact

No one is sure how Cuba got its name. It may have come from the Taíno people, who called it coabana, meaning "great place."

Fidel Castro, shown here, and his supporters easily took Cuba once Fulgencio Batista left the country.

WHAT IS COMMUNISM?

Communism is a government and an economic system in which goods are owned publicly rather than privately. In an ideal communist system, people work to their abilities and receive goods according to their needs. This is different from capitalism, in which a country's goods and trade are controlled by private owners. In action, however, the economies of communist countries have failed to provide for the needs of their people and share wealth in a fair way. Today, Cuba, China, North Korea, Laos, and Vietnam are the only communist countries that remain. None are wholly communist, however, allowing some private or semi-private businesses.

Fast Fact

Fidel Castro declared that Cuba would never be ruled by a dictator again. However, he, too, became a kind of dictator, not allowing political opposition and jailing enemies.

Fulgencio Batista, a soldier, became the leader of Cuba from 1933 to 1944. At first, he created an effective government and made improvements to the country. However, when Batista led Cuba again from 1952 to 1959, he became a dictator. He had total power, which he abused to become wealthy.

Fidel Castro grew up working in Cuba's sugarcane fields. He later became a lawyer, opening a practice for poor Cubans. Castro and his brother Raúl were against Batista and fought alongside others in a revolution

Raúl Castro stepped down as Cuba's president in April 2018. For the first time in 60 years, someone who wasn't a Castro led Cuba—Miguel Díaz-Canel Bermúdez.

Cuba

Raúl Castro

that successfully overthrew him in 1959. After Batista fled Cuba, Fidel Castro took control of the country, setting up a system of communism. Some Cubans hoped communism would end their hardships, while others were opposed to it.

A Shift in Power

Because the United States was against communism, it stopped trading with Cuba. In 1962, the U.S. government threatened Cuba after discovering **missiles** from the communist Soviet Union there. Eventually, the Soviet Union agreed to remove the missiles. Cuba lost a valuable **ally** when the Soviet Union dissolved in 1991.

Fidel Castro served as the prime minister, president, and commander of the armed forces of Cuba for nearly 50 years. In 2008, health issues caused him to step down and hand power over to his brother Raúl. Relations between Cuba and the United States started to improve. In 2015, the United States reopened its Cuban **embassy**. Cuba did the same with its embassy in the United States.

In 2019, Cubans ratified, or approved, a new constitution with some changes to the government, including establishing term limits for the president and recognizing private property. The same year, the government raised wages for those in some jobs, such as teachers and health-care workers. More reforms and measures to battle the country's economic troubles are expected in the future.

Carnival in Cuba likely evolved out of summer harvest festivals. Street performances are a popular part of the celebrations.

Chapter Three

TRADITIONS IN CUBA

A nation's holidays reveal a lot about its culture and history. Each year in Cuba, people remember the events of July 26, 1953. It was on this day that the Castro brothers and other **rebels** attacked two army bases in Santiago de Cuba. They hoped to overthrow the government of Fulgencio Batista then, but failed. However, years later, this was seen as the beginning of the end of Batista's dictatorship. In 1976, July 25, 26, and 27 were made Revolution Day holidays.

Other important state holidays include January 1, which is called the Triumph of the Revolution (or Liberation Day), and October 10, which is celebrated in remembrance of the day in 1868 that Cubans began to fight for freedom from Spain.

Cuba also celebrates a summer festival called Carnival (or Carnaval) in July. It includes parades, music, and dancing. Performers wear elaborate costumes. The Carnival in the city of Santiago de Cuba is the most famous of all.

Fast Fact

On October 10, 1868, near the town of Yara, Cuban lawyer Carlos Manuel de Céspedes freed his enslaved workers and invited them to fight for independence from Spain with the Grito de Yara ("Shout of Yara"). This day is still honored in Cuba.

RELIGION IN CUBA

Before the communist revolution, much of the Cuban population identified as Roman Catholic. Under Fidel Castro, religious leaders were sent out of the country, and religious schools were closed. There was a fear of churches supporting anti-communists. Christmas was removed as a national holiday. However, gradually, some religious freedoms were given back to Cuban citizens over the years. Christmas was made a national holiday again in 1997. Today, Santería, a religion of West African origin, is also practiced by many and is an important part of Cuban culture.

Traditional Cooking

Cuban meals tend to be a mix of African, Spanish, and other Caribbean traditional cuisines, or styles of cooking. Many dishes include rice and beans. Sandwiches, soups, and stews are also popular.

Criollo is a cuisine that's popular in many Hispanic countries, including Cuba. Criollo cooking combines meat—such as chicken, beef, or pork—with rice, beans, vegetables, and spices.

Fast Fact

Amid the COVID-19 pandemic, rising prices around the world meant even less food in Cuba. This led many Cubans to take part in protests in 2021.

Served as a side or a main dish, black beans and rice is a Cuban classic. The recipe starts with a sofrito.

A sauce called sofrito (which means "lightly fried") is made with a base of onions, garlic, and bell peppers. Tomatoes and meat may be added. Every cook's sofrito is a bit different.

Due to government rules and limits on trade, there are sometimes food shortages in Cuba. Certain foods, such as meats, can be hard to find. Cuba imports about 70 percent of its food.

Clothing in Cuba

The people of Cuba today mostly wear modern Western clothing. Men wear comfortable pants or shorts with a loose-fitting top or T-shirt.

The guayabera shirt is shown here. On the next page is an example of traditional Cuban women's clothing.

Fast Fact

In 2010, the Cuban government announced that the guayabera was the country's official formal dress shirt.

Women may wear skirts or dresses. The clothing is lightweight, often made from cotton or linen, to keep people cool.

Some special occasions, such as weddings or festivals, call for traditional dress, which is a reflection of Spanish and African styles. Cuban women may put on a layered skirt and bright top with embroidery. Headwraps are another popular choice. Rumba dresses, named for a style of Cuban music and dance, are vibrantly colored with many ruffles. Cuban men might wear a guayabera shirt, which has two or four pockets and pleats down the front and back.

The Gran Teatro de La Habana Alicia Alonso ("Grand Theatre of Havana Alicia Alonso"), in the heart of Havana, is the nation's most respected location for opera, ballet, and other performing arts.

THE ARTS

The Cuban government supports the arts, but in the past, it **censored** art if the work was thought to pose a threat. In recent years, the growing popularity of Cuban art in other places, including the United States and Europe, is bringing money into Cuba. This has led the government to loosen some restrictions.

Today, more than 200 neighborhood cultural centers, or *casas de culturas*, are found throughout Cuba. They offer workshops for people who are interested in all types of art. The government encourages talented artists and has set up the Cuban Film Institute, the National School for the Arts, and the National Cultural Council as ways to support them.

Fast Fact

The Ballet Nacional de Cuba ("Cuban National Ballet") was established in 1948 by the country's most famous ballet dancer—Alicia Alonso. The Gran Teatro de La Habana Alicia Alonso is named for her.

Cuban Cinema

Each year in December since 1979, Cuba hosts the Festival Internacional del Nuevo Cine Latinoamericano de La Habana ("International Festival of New Latin American Cinema of Havana"), or simply the

Havana Film Festival. The event promotes artistic films that explore the Latin American and Caribbean identity.

Many people in Cuba enjoy going to the cinema, or movie theater. Some cinema tickets cost less than 1 U.S. dollar because the government tightly controls film prices, production, and theaters.

Music and Dance

Music and dance have always been important to the people of Cuba. Traditional and modern styles suggest the influence of Spanish and African cultural heritage. Afro-Cuban music has become a symbol of national identity.

There are a number of popular musical styles in Cuba, including son and rumba. Son, or son cubano, usually features African

Street musicians play in parks throughout Cuban cities. Cuba hosts many music festivals throughout the year, including hip-hop, jazz, and classical events.

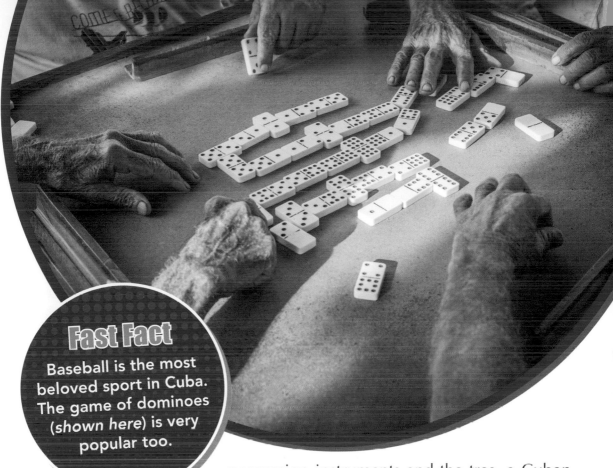

percussion instruments and the tres, a Cuban musical instrument related to the Spanish guitar. Son music often has themes of patriotism and love.

Rumba is a popular, upbeat style of music highlighting drumbeats that people dance to. "Rumba" may come from the verb *rumbear*, which means something like "to party" or "to have a good time" in Spanish.

Literature

Many types of literature are popular in Cuba. José Martí (1853–1895) was a poet who promoted freedom in his writings. His work inspired others to write about winning independence from Spain. Nicolás Guillén

CUBANS IN MIAMI

When Fidel Castro rose to power in 1959, a number of wealthy Cubans left the country. Many went to Miami, the second-largest city in Florida. Today, Miami is a busy urban center with a strong Cuban presence and influence. The neighborhood of Little Havana (*right*) is a hub of Latino culture and features the sights, sounds, and flavors of Cuba throughout its streets. Founded in 2000, Viernes Culturales, or Cultural Fridays, are held in Little Havana on the last Friday of every month to celebrate the vibrant culture of the neighborhood.

Fast Fact

Cuban writer Reinaldo Arenas (1943–1990) was jailed for challenging Fidel Castro. After failing to escape on an inner tube, he arrived in the United States in 1980 through the mass **migration** called the Mariel boatlift.

This is a statue of Ernest Hemingway, an American writer who lived in Cuba. His 1952 novel *The Old Man and the Sea* is set there.

(1902–1989), an **activist** poet, was the national poet of Cuba. He played a role in the creation of Afro-Cuban literature. Daína Chaviano (who was born in 1957), who now lives in the United States, is the most famous author of science fiction in Cuba.

Sharing Cuban culture with the world is sometimes difficult due to different governments' restrictions. Hopefully, in the future, Cubans will be able to more freely express their cultural traditions and themselves.

NEED-TO-KNOW INFO

Kind of Government
socialist republic (communist)

Population
11,116,396
(estimate, 2021)

Total Area
42,802 square miles
(110,857 sq km)

Capital City
Havana

Official Country Name
Republic of Cuba
(República de Cuba)

Kind of Money
Cuban peso

Oldest City
Baracoa (1511)

Flag

Location

THINK ABOUT IT!

1. Why do you think the religion of Santería remained part of Cuban culture?

2. How can food be considered a part of a people's culture?

3. Why do you think the Cuban communist government was worried about letting artists express themselves?

4. Why might Cuban Americans continue to celebrate their culture despite moving away from Cuba?

GLOSSARY

activist: Someone who acts strongly in support of or against an issue.

ally: A person or country associated with another for a common purpose.

cay: A small, low island or reef, usually sandy.

censor: To change or cut parts of something or ban something entirely after examining it.

embassy: The residence or offices of an official representative of a country in another country.

gender-neutral: Not referring specifically to gender.

heritage: The traditions and beliefs that are part of the history of a group or nation.

indigenous: The first people of an area.

islet: A small island, often rocky with little plant life.

migration: The act of moving from one country or place to settle in another.

missile: An object that is shot or launched to strike something from a distance.

pandemic: An outbreak of a disease that occurs over a wide area.

rebel: Someone who fights against authority.

republic: A form of government in which the people elect representatives who run the government.

FIND OUT MORE

Books

Rechner, Amy. *Cuba*. Minnetonka, MN: Bellwether Media, 2020.

Snow, Peggy. *Explore Cuba: 12 Key Facts*. Mankato, MN: 12 Story Library, 2019.

Ziff, John. *Cuba Under the Castros*. Philadelphia, PA: Mason Crest, 2018.

Websites

Cuba
www.cia.gov/the-world-factbook/countries/cuba/
Find all the facts about Cuba you need to know.

Cuba Facts for Kids
www.sciencekids.co.nz/sciencefacts/countries/cuba.html
Check out this great review of important facts about Cuba.

***National Geographic Kids*: Cuba**
kids.nationalgeographic.com/geography/countries/article/cuba
See some colorful photos of this interesting country.

INDEX